ONLY THE RING FINGER KNOWS

By
SATORU KANNAGI

HOTARU ODAGIRI

June

CONTENTS

Translator
Sachiko Sato

Letterer
Igor Cabbab

Graphic Design / Layout
Fred Lui

Editor
Bambi Eloriaga

Graphic Design Assistant
Eric Rosenberger

Editor in Chief
Fred Lui

Publisher
Hikaru Sasahara

English Edition Published by
DIGITAL MANGA PUBLISHING
A division of DIGITAL MANGA, Inc.
1487 W. 178th Street, Suite 300
Gardena, CA 90248

www.dmpbooks.com

First Edition: August 2004
ISBN: 1-56970-980-7

5 7 9 10 8 6

Printed in China

HANDSOME
INTELLIGEN

TALL AND
POPULAR...

KIND AND
GENTLE TO
EVERYONE
HE MEETS...

HE'S
LIKE A
DIAGRAM
FOR THE
PERFECT
HUMAN
BEING...

Ring. ① その指だけが知っている

WHY?!

WHY AM I SO UNLUCKY?!

NO, THAT'S *NOT* THE POINT!

WHY DOES HE EXIST IN SOME REGULAR OLD PRIVATE SCHOOL LIKE OURS...

AND AN UPPER-CLASSMAN, OF ALL THINGS!

WHY IN THE WORLD...

...ARE THERE *PERFECT* BEINGS LIKE THAT *KAZUKI?!*

HUH?

wAAAAAHHHHH

THE POINT IS...

I'M IN LOVE WITH UPPER-CLASSMAN KAZUKI... ♡

SIGH!

AND THE REASON IS YUICHI KAZUKI.

HE WAS DUMPED TODAY.

BY MAI TACHIBANA, THE CLASS HOTTIE.

I'M SORRY, BUT...

MAN, KAWAMURA'S A WRECK...

THERE'S A REASON FOR KAWAMURA'S BAD MOOD.

IN KAWAMURA'S ROOM

FORCED TO JOIN DRINKING BINGE.

GULP! GULP!

.....

DAMN! IT'S ALL THAT GUY'S FAULT!

BUT...

THOUGH YOU MIGHT THINK HE'D HAVE ALL KINDS OF GRUDGES LIKE THIS AGAINST HIM,

BUT I ALSO FEEL FOR YUICHI KAZUKI, BEGRUDGED JUST FOR EXISTING...

I UNDER-STAND HOW KAWAMURA FEELS...

STRANGELY ENOUGH,

THERE IS HARDLY ANY WHO SPEAKS BADLY OF YUICHI KAZUKI.

IT WAS THE SAME WITH ME.

THE YUICHI KAZUKI I SAW FROM AFAR...

...ALWAYS WORE A **GENTLE SMILE.**

HE DOESN'T HAVE ANY **WEIRD** FRIENDS, EITHER.

CAN'T TELL KAWAMURA THIS, BUT... ◊

AND THE PEOPLE AROUND HIM TREAT HIM **NORMALLY...**

HE DOESN'T **SEEM** LIKE A SNOB.

...AND I RATHER **LIKE** HIM.

YUP, THAT'S RIGHT. **THE RINGS.** THEY'RE ALL THE RAGE IN OUR SCHOOL.

HA HA

WHA..?! NO WAY...

THOSE...

AND I BOUGHT THESE MATCHING RINGS FOR **NOTHING...**

ARRRGH...!!

A WASTE...

WHAT?! STILL THINKING THAT...?

IF IT WASN'T FOR THAT YUICHI KAZUKI!!!!!

IF THINGS HAD GONE ACCORDING TO PLAN, I WOULD HAVE GOTTEN MAI...

LUCKY YOU...

...AND WE WOULD NOW BE GAZING LOVINGLY AT OUR PAIRED RINGS...

KAWAMURA RANTED ON AND ON...

I'LL KEEP YOU COMPANY.

LET'S DRINK TONIGHT.

OK, OK.

...BUT I DIDN'T REALLY THINK BADLY OF YUICHI KAZUKI!...

URRRRGHH! DAMN!

OK, OK.

...UNTIL THEN.

THE GUY WE TALKED ABOUT ALL NIGHT IS RIGHT IN FRONT OF ME!

TALK ABOUT AWKWARD!

ME! AND HE'S EVEN LENDING ME HIS HANDKERCHIEF!

UMMM...

UHHHH...

I'VE **NEVER** BEEN TREATED SO CASUALLY BY SOMEONE I HAVEN'T EVEN MET BEFORE.

AND BY AN UNDER-CLASSMAN, NO LESS.

HMPH!

UH, NO, I...

CRAP

I'M ORRY...

HUH?... HIS EXPRESSION...

WATARU FUJII!

DON'T FORGET IT!

W... WELL...!

URGH!

...AND?

...I...I MEAN... I HAVE A *NAME!*

FINE.

THIS IS FOR WATARU FUJII.

W... WHAT

YEAH... ...THAT IS WEIRD.

BUT CAN PEOPLE GAIN THAT MUCH WEIGHT SO SUDDENLY?

NO. BUT A RING **CAN'T** SUDDENLY SHRINK, EITHER...

S...

WHAAAA? WEREN'T YOU WEARING IT THIS MORNING?

YEAH...BUT IT SHOULD FIT MY **MIDDLE FINGER** AND NOW IT'S TOO TIGHT...

IT FITS MY **RING FINGER** THOUGH... **WEIRD.**

SEE?

WHOAA!!!

WHAA? **WHY?**

MURMUR,

MURMUR

EEK!

NO WAY...

HEY, LOOK...

MURMUR

WHA...

MURMUR,

MURMUR,

WH... WHAT'S GOING ON?

H...HEY!

28

...THE RINGS WERE **SWITCHED**.

BUT GOOD JOB YOU NOTICED THAT...

THE BEAUTIFUL ARE **LUCKY**.

...I **ALREADY** KNOW THAT.

THAT SAME RING LOOKS **DIFFERENT** ON HIM, WATARU.

HO OOOH

IT LOOKS **CLASSIER**.

MOST PEOPLE WOULD REALIZE IT THE MINUTE THEY TRIED IT ON.

IT DIDN'T EVEN OCCUR TO ME.

I THOUGHT MAYBE I GOT FAT...

THE RING LOOKS GOOD ON **HIM**.

WHAT!

...AND **YOU** WERE THE ONLY ONE NEXT TO ME.

THE ONLY TIME I REMOVED THIS WAS AT THE WATER FOUNTAIN...

DUMMY...

DUM..!

I BELIEVED HIM TOO.

WHAT ARE YOU, A **DUMMY?**

TO THINK THAT IN HALF A DAY YOU GOT FAT...

ON ME, IT WAS **LOOSE** ON MY RIGHT MIDDLE FINGER.

IT WAS **TIGHT** ON YOU, RIGHT?

HE **CONTROLS** THE CONVERSATION.

HE SAYS WHAT HE WANTS TO SAY, THEN LEAVES...

WHAT WAS THAT?

MURMUR

HE'S GONE.

IN THE FIRST PLACE,

HE'S THE ONE THAT TOOK THE WRONG RING.

GEEZ...

AT LEAST **APOLOGIZE** BEFORE LEAVING...

WHY IS HIS ATTITUDE ALWAYS SO **HOSTILE**?

WHEN HE LENT ME HIS HANDKERCHIEF...

HE WAS SO **KIND**...

...AND ON TOP OF THAT, **RICH!**

HANDSOME, TALL, INTELLIGENT...

I HEAR MR.KAZUKI COMES FROM A FAMILY OF **DENTISTS.**

HE MIGHT JUST **IGNORE** IT.

ANYWAY, PLEASE TAKE CARE OF THAT FOR ME?

IF YOU HAVE A FRIEND LIKE THAT,

WHY DON'T YOU EVER BRING HIM OVER?

OOOOH, **WATARU!!**

SLAP

ON!

THERE'S A **LETTER** INSIDE...

...SO I THINK MR. KAZUKI WILL CONTACT HER.

HUH? REALLY?

THAT GUY'S **NOT** MY FRIEND!

THAT GUY PROBABLY GETS SO MANY GIFTS,

HE COULD **SELL** THEM FOR PROFIT.

FROM THAT NUANCE, I TOTALLY THOUGHT YOU WERE CLOSE!

YOU CALLED HIM **"THAT GUY"** SO FAMILIARLY...

HMMM

MMMM, BUT I'VE HEARD HE'S NOT THAT **CRUEL.**

WOMEN ARE SHARP...

ZING

44

...AND **STILL** KEEP THE GIFT. ISN'T THAT RUDE?

MOST GUYS WOULD JUST **IGNORE** THE WHOLE THING.

THEY SAY THAT FOR **EVERY** LETTER OR PRESENT HE GETS,

HE GIVES EVERY GIRL A **PROPER** DECLINING ANSWER.

PRETTY COOL.

WHEN THEY HAVEN'T DONE ANYTHING WRONG.

AND TURNING SOMEONE DOWN IS PRETTY **STRESSFUL.**

THEY CRY AND STUFF.

THERE AREN'T MANY GUYS WHO'D APOLOGIZE AND SAY "SORRY",

YOU UNDERSTAND, DON'T YOU, WATARU?

YOU DECLINE A LOT OF THINGS.

....

URRGH!

PINNNKY PROOOMISE

WHY IS IT THAT I CAN **NEVER** SAY "NO" TO HER...?!

SO ANYWAY, IT'S A **DEAL!**

PINKY PROMISE! ♡

45

THIS IS DEFINITELY **NOT** A GOOD SITUATION!

I'M SORRY, TACHIBANA...

I'M SURE YOU UNDERSTAND...

...NOT GOOD.

THE **GUILT**...

I CAN'T GO OUT NOW THAT I'VE HIDDEN MYSELF...

URRGH...

WHY DID I HAVE TO **SNEAK** AFTER KAZUKI LIKE THIS...

HIS KIND VOICE,

HIS SOFT GAZE,

...CAN'T TELL KAWAMURA...

MAI TACHIBANA CONFESSING HER LOVE TO KAZUKI...

I WONDERED WHAT BUSINESS HE HAD AFTER SCHOOL IN A PLACE LIKE THIS...

AND YET, A **FIRM** ATTITUDE THAT LEAVES NO ROOM FOR ARGUMENT.

CRAP

I GUESS HE'S NOT POPULAR FOR NOTHING.

EVEN KAZUKI'S REJECTION WAS FLAWLESS...

BUT... LISTENING TO THE CONVERSATION,

FANCY MEETING *YOU* HERE.

WHAT'RE YOU DOING...

AAAGH!!

BUMP

OWWWWWWWW!

NOT EVEN THE LEAST BIT *FAZED* BY A *WOMAN'S* TEARS...

HEY, WHAT'RE YOU DOING?

THE GIRL? SHE'S GONE HOME.

OGLE OGLE HUH!

BY THE WAY...

WHAT WERE YOU DOING HERE?

YOU...! EVERY TIME...!

ZING!

...HUH?

...CARRYING THAT *BIG* PACKAGE MAKES YOU LOOK EVEN *SMALLER*.

WATARU FUJII.

THE **ROUGH** WORDS.

THE **SEVERE** LOOK.

...

...

WHERE WAS THE CAPTIVATING SMILE...

I USED TO GLIMPSE...

WHERE HAS IT GONE...?

THE **KINDNESS** HE SUPPOSEDLY DOLED OUT TO EVERYONE...

IT TURNS OUT IT **ISN'T EQUAL** FOR ALL.

...NONE OF IT WAS EVER...

...DIRECTED AT ME.

WHAT DID I EVER...

...DO TO YOU...?

WHEN I THINK ABOUT THAT,

I FEEL...

...STRANGELY SAD.

Ring. 1 END

Ring. ② その指だけが知っている

FROM THE FIRST TIME WE MET,

THERE WAS NOTHING I COULD DO.

THE HONOR STUDENT WITH A REP FOR KINDNESS, YUICHI KAZUKI...

...BUT IT **BOTHERS** ME

THAT EVERYONE WILL THINK I BROUGHT KAZUKI,

A BIRTHDAY PRESENT...

AND I CAN'T WANDER THE HALLS FOREVER.

I KNOW THE LUNCH HOUR'S OVER.

...I KNOW THAT.

...

I DON'T KNOW WHY.

BUT WITH ME, HE'S **COLD** AND **HURTFUL** AND **ALOOF**.

"IS PEEPING A HOBBY OF YOURS?"

DON'T EVER FOLLOW ME AGAIN."

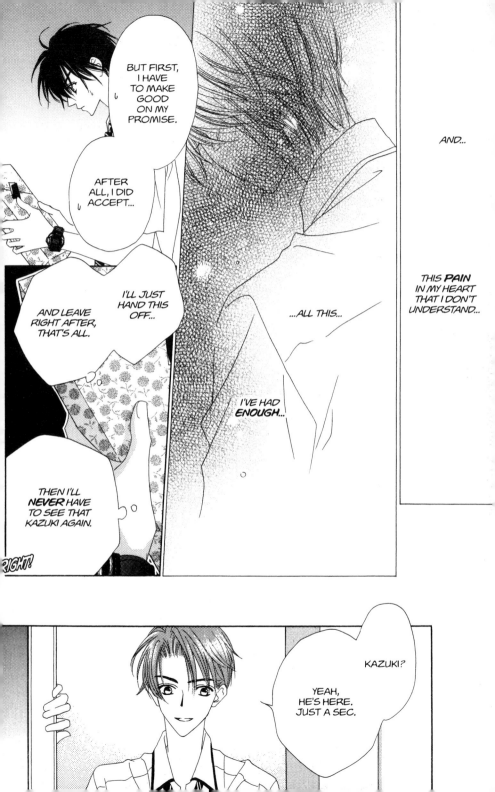

BUT FIRST, I HAVE TO MAKE GOOD ON MY PROMISE.

AFTER ALL, I DID ACCEPT...

I'LL JUST HAND THIS OFF...

AND LEAVE RIGHT AFTER, THAT'S ALL.

THEN I'LL **NEVER** HAVE TO SEE THAT KAZUKI AGAIN.

RIGHT!

AND...

THIS **PAIN** IN MY HEART THAT I DON'T UNDERSTAND...

...ALL THIS...

I'VE HAD **ENOUGH**...

KAZUKI?

YEAH, HE'S HERE. JUST A SEC.

WHA... I'M JUST...!!

YOU SURE YOU AREN'T... *FUNNY* THAT WAY?

YOU'VE BEEN ROAMING AROUND WITH THAT THING FOR QUITE A WHILE NOW, HAVEN'T YOU?

THIS IS HOW IT ALWAYS GOES!

W... WAIT...

WHAT? IS THERE SOMEONE IN THE SENIOR CLASS YOU WANT TO GIVE IT TO?

YOU WANT ME TO DELIVER IT FOR YOU?

NEVER HEARD MY REP?

HUH? HAVEN'T YOU HEARD? I'M A *NICE* GUY.

WH...WHAT CHANGED YOUR TUNE?

I WISH I'D *NEVER* KNOWN.

...HERE.

...THAT THE GUY STANDING IN FRONT OF ME WITH *COLD* EYES...

IS KIND TO EVERYONE *BUT ME...*

HMPH

I FORGOT ABOUT *THAT* THE MINUTE I MET YOU.

I WISH I REALLY COULD FORGET...

SHOVE

60

JUST NOW... WHAT WERE YOU...

...WHAT?

YOU SUDDENLY CLAMMED UP, I JUST WANTED TO SEE HOW YOU WOULD REACT.

ALL I DID WAS SAY YOUR NAME.

C... CUT IT OUT!

SLAP!

YOU COMPLAIN *TOO* MUCH. BESIDES...

I...I DIDN'T SAY THAT...

YOU'RE THE ONE THAT'S BEING OVERLY FAMILIAR WITH A SENIOR LIKE ME.

WHAT, DID YOU THINK I WAS GONNA **KISS** YOU OR SOMETHING?

D...DON'T GET **FAMILIAR** WITH ME!

WHAT HAPPENED TO YOUR ATTITUDE, WATARU?

HMMM... EVEN THOUGH YOU'RE **BLUSHING**?

...WHAT DOES THAT HAVE TO DO WITH THIS?

EVERYTHING!

LIKE, THERE'S THIS **COLD** SIDE OF YOU, YOU KNOW?

YOU'VE ALWAYS BEEN LIKE THIS, WATARU.

WATARU, WHAT **DID** YOU DO?! I **TOTALLY** LOST FACE!!

I BET YOU'VE **NEVER** EVEN SERIOUSLY FELT LOVE FOR ANYONE BEFORE.

SAYING YOU **WEREN'T SURE** IF YOU REALLY LOVED HER OR NOT.

EVEN WITH NANO, YOU SUDDENLY BROKE UP WITH HER...

A MAN THAT WON'T LET YOU HAVE ANY FANTASIES ABOUT HIM IS NO MAN AT ALL!

HMPH!

SCARY...

KARIN, THAT GUY...

HE'S **NOT** THE GREAT GUY YOU ALL THINK HE IS, YOU KNOW?

ISN'T THAT WHY YOU'RE SO INDIFFERENT?!

BAM!

MAYBE...

HE SHOWED SUCH EMOTION BECAUSE...

...HE THOUGHT THE PRESENT WAS FROM ME.

MAYBE I'M TOTALLY WRONG, BUT...

NO...IT CAN'T BE...

BUT...

IS IT... ME?

MAYBE HE DOESN'T HATE ME SO MUCH AFTER ALL.

IF THAT'S TRUE, THEN...

HE PROBABLY WOULDN'T GIVE ME AN ANSWER.

THIS IS THE LAST ONE.

EVEN IF I WANTED...

TO CONFIRM SUCH A THING...

MAYBE HE REEAALLY LIKES YOU, WATARU?

BUT...

LOOK AT THIS **CROWD**...

OOH HEY!

WE'RE **WINNING!**

...FOR A CHANGE

THERE'S KAZUKI.

UH...

HUFF...

THMP

HE JUST LEFT.

HE...

NO... WHY ISN'T HE HERE?

WHAT...

WHERE DID YOU GO...?

HUFF...

KAZUKI...!

...LOOKING FOR ME?

WHUSHH

Ring. ②END

その指だけが知っている

Ring. ③

I THOUGHT I DIDN'T WANT ANYTHING TO DO WITH HIM.

KAZUKI...?

THAT'S **SIR** KAZUKI TO YOU.

BUT...

I RAN AFTER HIM **INSTINCTIVELY.**

IF I TURN AND LOOK NOW...

SHK

SHK

THE GAME SHOULD BE OVER SOON.

THEY'RE WINNING BECAUSE OF YOU.

WHY ARE YOU BEING SO INCONSIDERATE?

WHAT?

YOU *DON'T* FOOL ME...

I BET THE TEAM WANTS YOU TO PLAY THROUGH *TILL* THE END.

YOU WERE PLANNING TO LEAVE BEFORE THE END ALL ALONG.

THE GAME.

THE CONTRAST FITS YOUR PERSONALITY TO A "T"

SMALL BODY, CLUNKY HI-TOPS...

THOSE ARE COOL.

FROM THE CHEERS, I'D SAY WE **WON**.

HUH?

STAND

YEAH...

WHAT'S THAT SUPPOSED TO MEAN?

THAT YOU'RE **ROUGH** AND **UNREFINED**.

AM I BEING MOCKED AGAIN...?

AND **THAT** IS A MOST PREDICTABLE RESPONSE.

HA HA

....!

J...JUST TO LET YOU KNOW, I'M **NEVER** TAKING THIS RING OFF AGAIN!

I CAME RUNNING OUT BECAUSE I WAS **WORRIED** ABOUT HIM...

IT WAS **FINALLY** GOING WELL...

SO OF COURSE I'LL **NEVER** LOSE IT, EITHER!

I HAVE **MORE** OF AN **ATTACHMENT** TO THIS RING THAN YOU'LL EVER HAVE...

AND THE FACT THAT WE HAVE THE SAME DESIGN **REALLY** GETS ON MY **NERVES!**

SO I PRAY THAT WITH EVERY PASSING DAY, YOU'LL GET **TIRED** OF YOURS!

AND IT JUST MADE ME LOOK LIKE A **FOOL!**

BUT IN THE END, HE ACTS LIKE IT'S ALL A **BIG JOKE!**

NO...

ダッ ダッ

YAAY, WE WON!

RAAAHH

....

NO.

THIS IS **NOT** WHAT I WANT TO SAY...

BUT IF I **DON'T** ACT THIS WAY,

KAZUKI MIGHT FIND OUT...

THE CROWD'S PILING OUT...

WELL... I'M LEAVING NOW.

...THAT I FELT LIKE HIS RING WAS MINE'S **OTHER HALF**...

GRIP

HE KISSED...

THAT JERK...!

MY RING...!

HE'S JUST MAKING FUN OF ME!

HUH?!

WHERE'D HE GO?

DAMN! IT'S ALWAYS LIKE THIS!

HE SAYS WHAT HE WANTS TO SAY, DOES WHAT HE WANTS TO DO...

LEAVES ME RILED AND DISAPPEARS...!

WHAT DOES HE MEAN, "SERVES YOU RIGHT"?

AND ALSO BECAUSE...

AND THE FACT THAT WE HAVE THE SAME DESIGN **REALLY** GETS ON MY NERVES!

WHY...

WOULD HE DO THAT...

MAYBE...

I'M THE **OWNER** OF IT...?

HE FEELS THAT WAY TOO.

"MAYBE...

...HE **REEAALLY** HATES YOU, WATARU?"

₣"
ち
'
CLENCH!

UM...

THE RUMOR THAT YOUR **SISTER** IS SEEING MR.KAZUKI...

...IS IT **TRUE**...?

AGAIN...

THANKS TO IT ALL, I GET CALLED OUT LIKE THIS ON A DAILY BASIS.

SHE'S A FRESH-MAN...

SO THIS GIRL LIKES KAZUKI **TOO**...

I NEVER THOUGHT...

...KAWAMURA'S PLOT WOULD GO THIS WELL.

THE STORY THAT "KAZUKI CAME TO ASK ABOUT FUJII'S SISTER'S SCHOOL" BECAME...

..."KAZUKI IS **DATING** FUJII'S SISTER"

THOSE TWO...

I DON'T REALLY KNOW...

ALL TOO EASILY.

THAT TIME...

IT'S TRUE THAT I FELT **FLUSHED**...

THERE'S GOTTA BE SOMETHING **WRONG** WITH ME.

...THINKING OF **HIM** AS A SUBJECT FOR ROMANCE...

SCRUNCH

BUT THAT'S NOT PROOF THAT I'M IN LOVE WITH HIM..:

WHSSH...

IN SPRING,

THESE CHERRY BLOSSOMS BLOOM AND IT'S **BEAUTIFUL** HERE.

SIGH GREENERY IS SO CALMING...

AND YET, I FEEL LIKE WE'VE KNOWN EACH OTHER SINCE WE WERE LITTLE...

AND HE FEELS **SPECIAL** TO ME SOMEHOW.

IT'S BEEN LESS THAN TWO WEEKS SINCE WE FIRST STARTED TALKING...

THERE... REALLY IS SOMETHING **WRONG** WITH ME.

IF KAZUK_ WERE T_ WALK HER_ THROUG_ _A RAIN O_ CHERRY BLOSSOM_

I BET IT WOULD BE **PICTURE-PERFECT.**

THAT'S RIGHT...

TOMORROW... SUNDAY'S SUPPOSED TO BE HIS **BIRTHDAY.**

...
...

OH YEAH, BUT BY SPRING OF NEXT YEAR, HE'LL BE GRADUATING...

OH, THERE'S ONIONS IN IT, BUT...

...I'LL TAKE OUT THE ONES IN YOUR PORTION, OK?

...IN A GOOD MOOD?

OK...

I'M LATE.

I'M HOME...

I'M HOME...

CLICK

OHHH HEY, *THANK YOU*, WATARU.

HUH?

CLICK

TONIGHT,

YOU FOLLOWED UP ON THAT BUSINESS WITH MR. KAZUKI FOR ME, RIGHT?

IT'S WATARU'S *FAVORITE*!

WELCOME HOME, WATARU!

I'M MAKING DINNER NOW.

CHILLED PASTA WITH CLAMS AND MINESTRONE. ♡

HE SAID, "YOU'RE MISS KARIN OF FIRST YEAR, RIGHT?"

TODAY...

HA HA

MR. KAZUKI CAME DOWN TO MY SCHOOL!

FOLLOW UP...?

ABOUT WHAT?

PANG!

THAT'S RIGHT... I TOTALLY FORGOT...

KAZUKI...? AT **YOUR** SCHOOL...?

HE CAME TO ASK ABOUT KARIN'S SCHOOL...

I THINK HE WAITED BY THE SCHOOL GATE UNTIL I CAME OUT... ♡

KARIN HAS NO IDEA...

MY HEART ACHES...

THE PERSON WHO MOST RESENTED THE RUMOR ABOUT KAZUKI AND KARIN... WAS **ME**.

...THAT AT MY SCHOOL, SHE'S KNOWN AS KAZUKI'S LOVE INTEREST...

I SEE.

HE MUST'VE CUT FOURTH PERIOD, OTHERWISE...

THERE COULDN'T HAVE BEEN SUCH GOOD TIMING.

I'M SO MOVED ♪♪

I FINALLY GET IT.

OR HAVE YOU ALREADY **CONFESSED?**

AT THIS RATE, IT MUST ALL BE CLEAR TO MR. KAZUKI BY NOW.

YOU'RE **SO** EASY TO READ!

DOWN BOY, DON'T GET EXCITED.

FEELINGS, WHAT FEELINGS...?!

F...!

ACTUALLY, I WAS A BIT SUSPICIOUS.

I THOUGHT MAYBE YOUR OWN FEELINGS WERE GETTING **IN THE WAY** OF DELIVERING THAT PRESENT.

WHA...

JEALOUS...?

"YOU..."

THINK **RATIONALLY!**

OF...OF...OF COURSE NOT! HE'S A **GUY!**

MR. KAZUKI POLITELY DECLINED, AS USUAL, ON THE SPOT.

YOU'RE THE **ONE** WHO HAS TO BE RATIONAL, WATARU!

OOOOH

HE... **DECLINED...**

THERE, DO YOU FEEL BETTER NOW?

I... I'M...

TO BE HONEST, I DON'T EVEN UNDERSTAND MY OWN FEELINGS YET.

SO IT'S NOT THAT FAR FROM MY HOUSE...

I NEVER EVEN IMAGINED THAT I WOULD FALL IN LOVE WITH ANOTHER MAN.

I **WANT** TO SEE KAZUKI AND TALK TO HIM.

AND THERE'S STILL A PART OF ME...

...THAT DOESN'T WANT TO ACCEPT IT.

LET'S SEE... FIFTH STREET.

I GUESS IT'S THEIR ANNUAL CUSTOM.

APPARENTLY, HE'S SPENDING HIS BIRTHDAY AT HIS FAMILY'S HOUSE.

THEIR RELATIVES COME AND IT'S A BIG FUSS.

IF I COULD JUST SEE KAZUKI'S FACE...

HIGH SOCIETY

IT'S RIGHT THERE IF I CUT THROUGH THIS PARK.

EVEN BEFORE *EARNING* KAZUKI'S LOVE,

OR FINDING OUT IF OUR FEELINGS ARE *MUTUAL*...

I WANT TO KNOW MY OWN *TRUE FEELINGS* FIRST.

AT ANY RATE...

...THIS FOG MIGHT LIFT.

IF I COULD MEET HIM AND BE *CERTAIN*... ALTHOUGH I STILL DON'T KNOW...

...WHAT I'LL DO AFTER THAT...

WHEN I WAS WITH NANO,

MY HEART WAS FILLED WITH *CALM*.

AND I THOUGHT THAT WAS *LOVE*.

WHEN I'M DEALING WITH KAZUKI, IT DOESN'T GO THAT WAY AT ALL.

BEING NERVOUS HAS MADE ME THIRSTY...

I NEED WATER...

AS TIME WENT ON, I STARTED TO FEEL *OUT OF PLACE* WITH THIS CALM.

BUT...

IT'S MUCH QUICKER IF WE CUT THROUGH HERE.

NO MATTER HOW MANY TIMES YOU COME OVER, YOU STILL FORGET.

NO, NO, TOUKO...

IT'S AN EMOTIONAL ROLLER-COASTER...

ANGER...

SURPRISE...

WHY...? HE'S SUPPOSED TO BE AT HOME CELEBRATING WITH HIS FAMILY...

AND WHO'S THAT WOMAN WITH HIM...?

SHE'S AT LEAST THREE OR FOUR YEARS OLDER...

I KNOW.

OK, OK.

K...KAZUKI...!

HIDES INSTINCTIVELY.

WELL EXCUSE ME!

AND NO MATTER HOW MANY TIMES I COME OVER, YOU'RE STILL RUDE, YUICHI.

JUST LIKE THE END OF THIS FEELING...

THERE IS ONLY THE **BITTER** TASTE OF SILVER WHERE THE RING USED TO BE.

SHE SAID SHE CAME BY CAR,

SO I'LL PROBABLY NEVER SEE HER AGAIN.

I GUESS **PARTINGS** ARE ALWAYS THIS **ANTI-CLIMACTIC**...

Ring. 3 END

Ring. ④

SKY BLUE ⑲

YOU WENT TO HER SCHOOL... YOU EVEN CUT FOURTH PERIOD TO GO...

KARIN TOLD ME.

BUT...

YOU WENT TO SEE HER...

WHAT?

WHAT DO YOU MEAN...?

WHAT WERE YOU THINKING?

WHAT?

DOES IT HAVE SOMETHING TO DO WITH THE RUMOR?

IF IT DOES, THEN I...

WHAT *HAPPENED* ON YOUR BIRTHDAY?

I TOLD YOU, IT HAD NOTHING TO DO WITH YOU.

WATARU, YOUR BRAIN MUST BE REALLY *PUNY*.

わしゃ
RUMPLE

わしゃ
RUMPLE

ぐしゃっ
SCRUNCH

I... FEEL DIZZY...

HF...

IT'S ROUGH...

I'LL BE OKAY, KAWAMURA...

THANKS.

THOUGH I KEEP MY DISTANCE,

MY THOUGHTS KEEP TAILING AFTER KAZUKI'S SHADOW.

AND WITH EVERY THOUGHT OF HIM, MY HEART *ACHES*...

I CAN'T EVEN EAT.

...IT'S *ROUGH*.

NO...

NOTHING...

IT'S A *LIE*.

PLEASE TAKE YOUR TIME.

S...SHE'S...

THE ONE WHO WAS WITH KAZUKI...

WHAT...

I THINK HER NAME WAS... "TOUKO"

TO MEET HER IN A PLACE LIKE THIS...

THERE'S NO MISTAKE.

IT'S HER.

AND WHAT ARE YOU LOOKING FOR TODAY?

WHY NOT LET YOUR **BOYFRIEND** SPOIL YOU AND GET SOMETHING EXPENSIVE?

SINCE IT'S YOUR BIRTHDAY...

OH.

NO, NO, HE'S NOT MY BOYFRIEND...

IT'S ONLY MY BROTHER, UNFORTUNATELY...

WELL RIGHT NOW, THERE ARE A LOT OF SILVER BANGLES OUT, BUT...

ARE YOU...

A STUDENT AT RYOKUYO HIGH?

HIS COUSIN...

EXCUSE ME, BUT...

THUMP

SO SHE IS A RELATIVE...

HUH? Y...**YES,** BUT...

BUT WHETHER SHE'S HIS COUSIN OR HIS SECOND COUSIN...

HUH...?

I'M HIS **COUSIN.**

THEN DO YOU KNOW A SENIOR NAMED **YUICHI KAZUKI?**

SHE'S STILL MUCH MORE OF A CANDIDATE FOR HIS LOVE INTEREST THAN I AM.

KARIN... YOU'RE USING THE **PAST TENSE...**

HE WAS... A **REALLY** GREAT MAN.

HE'S HELPED MY BROTHER OUT MANY TIMES.

WE KNOW MR. KAZUKI VERY WELL!

ACTUALLY, HE *IS* ACTING LIKE A DEAD PERSON.

...YOU'RE *RIGHT*.

I'M SO SORRY!

WHOOPS...

BUT

AS FAR AS YOU'RE CONCERNED, HE IS AS GOOD AS DEA...D...

HUH? YOU MEAN... MR. KAZUKI?

YES.

THAT BOY IS SO PROUD.

I'M SURE HE ACTS PERFECTLY NORMAL AT SCHOOL, BUT...

I'M TOLD HE'S ALMOST COMPLETELY STOPPED SPEAKING AT HOME.

HE DOESN'T EAT AND HE STAYS COOPED UP IN HIS ROOM...

A WEEK...

HEY

SOUND LIKE SOMEBODY YOU KNOW?

IT SEEMS HE'S BEEN LIKE THIS FOR AN ENTIRE WEEK.

POKE

POKE

AND YOU DON'T KNOW THE **CAUSE?**

YUICHI'S BROTHER IS MARRIED AND LIVES IN ANOTHER CITY...

I DON'T KNOW WHAT HAPPENED, BUT HIS PARENTS ARE BOTH **VERY** WORRIED...

...AND THEY CAME TO DISCUSS IT WITH ME.

YUICHI WON'T SAY A WORD.

WAS THERE ANYTHING AT SCHOOL? SOME TROUBLE...?

BUT HE AND I GREW UP TOGETHER...

...SO WE'RE LIKE **BROTHER AND SISTER.**

...TROUBLE...

OTHERS' EXPECTATIONS OF HIM ARE **HIGH,** TOO.

AND BECAUSE HE DOES SO WELL...

BUT SOMEHOW, I THINK THAT'S CAUSED A LOT OF **STRESS** FOR HIM.

THAT BOY...

EVER SINCE HE WAS A CHILD, HE'S BEEN GOOD WITH PEOPLE...

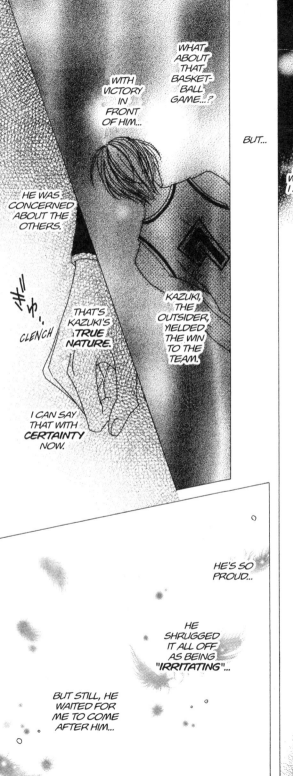

W...**WHEN** WAS THAT?!

THE SAME RING WORN BY THE PERSON HE LOVES...

THAT'S WHAT HE ASKED ME TO MAKE.

FOR HIM.

COULD IT BE THAT...

SHE MADE THAT RING...?

...AND AT KAZUKI'S **REQUEST?**

"TO OBTAIN IT, I HAD TO BE SO UNREASON-ABLE

AND HAVE MISS TOUKO MAKE A PRESENT OF IT FOR ME."

HUH?

UMM...

I THINK...

IT WAS AROUND THE TIME THE CHERRY BLOSSOMS STARTED FALLING, SO...

YES... ALL I KNOW IS THAT...

...IT'S SOMEONE AT HIS SCHOOL.

THE PERSON **HE** LOVES...?

THAT'S ABOUT THE SAME TIME THAT I FIRST LOST MY RING!

APRIL...

YOU KNOW...

THERE'S A LINE OF CHERRY TREES FROM THE STATION ALL THE WAY TO RYOKUYO HIGH SCHOOL, RIGHT?

HE ASKED ME RIGHT AFTER WE HAD GONE TO SEE THEM TOGETHER.

...I THINK IT WAS IN **APRIL...**

ANYWAY, KAZUKI'S ATTITUDE WAS ALWAYS ONE OF **ANIMOSITY** TOWARDS ME

AND THAT MADE ME **SAD**...

WAIT... BUT WASN'T HE SUPPOSED TO BE...

A **STUBBORN** AND **PROUD** AND **TROUBLESOME** GUY...?

THAT'S WHY I LASHED OUT AT HIM SO MANY TIMES.

AND HE WOULD JUST CALMLY TAKE IT...

IS KAZUKI SOMEHOW INVOLVED WITH THAT TOO...?

I DON'T KNOW...

I BOUGHT THAT RING AT SOME RANDOM STORE.

IT COULD BE ABOUT SOMEONE ELSE'S RING.

HUH?

UM...

EXCUSE ME,

DO YOU KNOW WHERE KAZUKI IS TODAY?

AND IT HAS TO BE **NOW**!

I WANT TO SEE HIM!

THERE'S SOMETHING I HAVE TO TALK TO HIM ABOUT...

KAZUKI...

...I FOUND A SNAPSHOT OF YOU AT THE SCHOOL FESTIVAL.

THEN, A FEW DAYS LATER I WAS PASSING THE TIME IN THE STUDENT COUNCIL OFFICE LOOKING THROUGH SCHOOL PICTURES WHEN...

OF COURSE I HAD NO IDEA WHO THE OWNER WAS...

...IT WAS A TOTAL *COINCIDENCE*...

AND TO BE HONEST, I DIDN'T MUCH CARE.

...THAT I FOUND THE RING.

YOU WERE WEARING THE RING THAT I'D FOUND.

BUT...

I SECRETLY PUT IT ON YOUR DESK...

TO SEE HOW YOU'D *REACT*.

SO...

IT'S A *GENERIC* RING... IT COULD'VE BEEN *ANYONE'S*, RIGHT?

ABOUT YOUR RING MOVING TO THE RING FINGER... AND ME GETTING MY RING BACK...

STARTING TOMORROW...

...THERE'S GONNA BE *MORE* RUMORS ABOUT US...

HMMM...

WHY DON'T WE JUST LET THEM SAY WHAT THEY WANNA SAY?

YEAH... I GUESS YOU'RE RIGHT.

...AND ANYWAY...

ONLY OUR RING FINGERS KNOW *THE TRUTH.*

Ring. 4 END

SQUEEZE

WIGGLE
WIGGLE

TAKAKO, WE'RE COMING IN.

CHAK

I HATE YOU!

HUMPH!

HUF
HUF

HEY TAKAKO...

UM...

I'M SORRY...

TAKING AWAY THE RING I GAVE YOU...

THE MAN FROM THE PARK...

YEAH.

UM...

HELLO? TAKAKO...?

OH...

SHE'S BEEN MAD AT ME EVER SINCE I TOOK THE RING FROM HER.

WHAT TO DO...

WHAT'S THIS...?

OH DEAR...

...THAT HE DOESN'T WANT YOU TO MARRY ME.

UNCLE YUICHI LOVES TAKAKO *SOOO* MUCH...

HUH?!

...

UM... WELL... YOU SEE...

IT'S LIKE THIS...

UNCLE YUICHI IS GOING TO MARRY ME?

SO DOES THAT MEAN...

SO I HAD TO GIVE YOU UP.

I'M SORRY...?

YOU...! WHAT ARE YOU...

SHH!

BACK-FIRED...

HEY...

AFTERWORD HOTARU ODAGIRI

SO READERS, WHICH BOY ARE YOU A FAN OF? WATARU OR YUICHI? I AM VERY MUCH A YUICHI FAN! (WHICH IS EASY TO UNDERSTAND...)

ONE DAY, MY EDITOR ASKED ME: "WOULDN'T YOU LIKE TO SEE A MOVING YUICHI!?" OF COURSE, I IMMEDIATELY REPLIED, "YEESSS!" AND SO, BECAUSE OF MY EDITOR'S BRILLIANT PSYCHOLOGICAL TACTICS AGAINST ME, I WAS PUT TO WORK ON THE PROJECT OF TURNING THIS STORY INTO A MANGA.

I WAS GREATLY THRILLED BY THE PHRASE, "A MOVING YUICHI." THE ONLY THING I FAILED TO GRASP WAS THE FACT THAT IT WOULD BE ME TASKED WITH ACCOMPLISHING THIS FEAT (I REALIZED IT TOO LATE).

WHILE WORKING ON THIS SERIES, I SUFFERED TREMENDOUS AGONIES. WITH MY LEVEL OF SKILL, I FELT THERE WAS NO WAY THAT I COULD ADEQUATELY PORTRAY YUICHI'S AMAZING APPEAL. OR, FOR THAT MATTER, WATARU'S EITHER. BUT NOW THAT IT'S OVER, LOOKING BACK, THE ONLY FEELING I HAVE LEFT WITHIN ME IS THAT "IT WAS FUN."

BEING A SLOWPOKE, EVEN WITH A SMALL WORKLOAD, I CAUSED PEOPLE TROUBLE BY ALWAYS SKIRTING ON THE CLIFF'S EDGE. EVERY ISSUE, DUE TO VARIOUS REASONS, WE WERE FORCED TO GET THE ARTWORK OUT WITH A VERY SMALL STAFF AND SOMETIMES, NEARLY KILLED OURSELVES WITH STRESS. BUT WE DID OUR BEST. THANK YOU VERY MUCH FOR ALLOWING ME TO DO THIS PROJECT.

IF YOU WOULD LIKE TO KNOW MORE ABOUT THESE TWO AFTER THEY BECAME A LOVING COUPLE, PLEASE DO READ ABOUT THEM IN MR. KANNAGI'S WONDERFUL NOVELS. IN THEM, YOU'LL FIND EPISODES THAT WE SADLY HAD TO CUT FROM THE MANGA DUE TO SPACE CONSTRAINTS. SO IF YOU HAVEN'T YET READ A COPY, PLEASE DO.

LASTLY, TO MY EDITOR, FOR ALWAYS PUTTING UP WITH MY RANTING AND WHINING DURING THIS SERIES, I THANK YOU (SOB). (CONTINUING EVEN AT PRESENT AND BEING A MAJOR NUISANCE...)

TO ALL THE PEOPLE WHO READ THIS, AND ALL THE PEOPLE WHO WROTE ME... A GREAT BIG THANK YOU! YOUR LETTERS REALLY ENCOURAGED ME. I WILL BE SENDING OUT REPLIES AND THINGS, SO PLEASE WAIT PATIENTLY FOR THEM.

★ COME TO THINK OF IT, THIS WILL BE MY TENTH COM HAVING BEEN AB TO COME THIS FA DESPITE MY SLO HAND, IT'S ALL THA TO YOU READERS HUGE THANK YO

HERE'S WATARU. ♪

Satoru Kannagi
Afterwords

First off, let me celebrate the release of the "...Ring Finger..." comic! And to all the readers who kindly bought this book, thank you very much.

When the offer for turning this story into a manga first came up, it didn't sink in right away. I remember just standing there like a zombie after I hung up the phone. I have gone through my works making the transition from magazine serial to novel, but to add the transformation into manga as well! On top of that, a series! There will never be enough thanks to go around.

But that was just the beginning. From the moment the series started, my hands shook with every turn of the page. I was always in suspense even though I wrote the story myself, and there wasn't a moment when I could read the manga calmly. This was especially true of the last episode. My heart almost exploded at the kissing scene in the student council room, and I was almost K.O.'d by Kazuki's smiling face in the final scenes...and so it went. If someone were watching me, it must have been a creepy sight indeed!

I would not say that Ms. Odagiri drew my story exactly as I imagined, but rather, she has made the series completely her own. As a fan/reader myself, I thoroughly enjoyed it to the very end. Her good taste shows in every little detail (such as Kazuki's and Wataru's way of wearing their uniforms, or their long, lovely fingers on which any ring would look perfect), and the girls in the story are all like fine sugar candy. I was filled with happiness looking at every inch of every frame. Since I didn't write this story with the intention of turning it into a manga, I expect that there must have been some difficulties encountered behind the scenes in the conversion... but at this time, I have only thanks and more thanks.

If there are those of you who are curious about these two and the progress of their relationship, please do check out the novels as well.

And now, I'd like to announce the winners of some special Kannagi awards: 1) Award for most wanting to play dress-up: "Takako Kazuki" 2) Award for most wanting to be petted and healed by: "Puru" 3) Award for most wanting to know what his first name is: "Kawamura". To these three, a warm "Thank you for all your work."

Satoru Kannagi

ONLY THE RING FINGER KNOWS

その指だけが知っている

Two Rings, One Love

The all time best selling yaoi manga returns as a novel!

Volume 1: The Lonely Ring Finger   ISBN: 1-56970-904-1 $8.95
Volume 2: The Left Hand Dreams of Him   ISBN: 1-56970-885-1 $8.95
Volume 3: The Ring Finger Falls Silent   ISBN: 1-56970-884-3 $8.95

New Novel Series!

by
Satoru Kannagi
Hotaru Odagiri

June

junemanga.co

TIME LAG

Love, through the lens of a camera...

Satoru, the class photographer and
Shirou , the school track star... Will
love bring them together?

June™

unemanga.com

ISBN#1-56970-921-1 $12.95

Time Lag © 1999, 2000 by Shinobu GOTOH and Hotaru ODAGIRI.
All rights reserved. Original Japanese edition
published by TOKUMA SHOTEN PUBLISHING CO., LTD.

YOU & HARUJION

by Keiko Kinoshita

All is lost...

Haru has just lost his father,
Yakuza-esque creditors are
coming to collect on his
father's debts, and the
bank has foreclosed
the mortgage on
the house...

When things go from bad to worse,
in steps Yuuji Senoh...

ISBN# 1-56970-925-4 $12.95

June™

junemanga.com

SAME CELL ORGANISM

by Sumomo Yumeka

Different... yet alike...

How can two people be so completely different from one another, yet be so in tune with love?

ISBN: 1-56970-926-2 $12.95

Same-Cell Organism/Dousaibou Seibutsu © Sumomo Yumeka 2001.
Originally published in Japan in 2001 by Taiyo Tosho Co., Ltd.

June™ by DMP
junemanga.com

When the music stops...
love begins.

Il gatto sul G

*Kind-hearted Atsushi finds Riya injured
on his doorstep and offers him a safe haven
from the demons pursuing him.*

By Tooko Miyagi

Vol. 1 ISBN# 1-56970-923-8 $12.95
Vol. 2 ISBN# 1-56970-893-2 $12.95

june™

junemanga.com

Don't Worry Mama

a novel

Stranded...

Yuichi and his spoiled boss, Imakura, are mistakenly left behind on a deserted island. Can they survive until someone notices they're missing?

One of the most popular "boy's love" stories returns as a novel, and includes a bonus story, "Present."

ISBN# 1-56970-886-X $8.95

June™

junemanga.com

Written and Illustrated by
You Higuri

A desperate search…

In the garden of the sacred beast…

Gorgeous Carat Galaxy

Danger awaits those who dare to enter.

ISBN# 1-56970-903-3 $12.95

Gorgeous Carat Galaxy © You Higur 2004. Originally published
in Japan in 2004 by GENTOSHA Comics Inc., Tokyo.

June

junemanga.co